Little Children's Bible Books

PAUL

*Retold by Anne de Graaf
Illustrated by José Pérez Montero*

BROADMAN
& HOLMAN
PUBLISHERS

Dedicated to
Pedro Pérez Rollán and YOU!

PAUL

Published in 2001 by Broadman & Holman Publishers,
Nashville, Tennessee

Text copyright © 2001 Anne de Graaf
Illustration copyright © 2001 José Pérez Montero
Design by Ben Alex
Conceived, designed and produced by Scandinavia Publishing House
Printed in Hong Kong
ISBN 0-8054-2194-7

Saul was someone
who hurt Jesus' friends.

7

Then one day a bright light knocked him right off his horse and blinded him.

Cover your eyes. That's how Saul felt.

Saul heard Jesus' voice,
"When you hurt my followers,
you hurt me."

Take your hands off your eyes. You can see where you're going. That's how Saul felt when God helped him to see that Jesus is the Son of God.

Then Jesus helped Saul to see again, and gave him a new name. From then on he was called Paul. After his change of heart, Paul traveled far and wide, telling everyone he met about Jesus' love.

Greece and Turkey are two of the countries Paul visited. Can you find them on a map?

14

Paul made many journeys to talk to people about believing in Jesus. Sometimes he went alone, and sometimes with his friends Silas and Timothy.

Who do you go on trips with? What do you pack when you travel?

Jesus' enemies threw Paul and Silas into prison. But Paul and Silas could still pray and sing songs about God's love inside prison.

Jesus' enemies arrested Paul. Because of this, he had to go to Rome, in Italy, and he had to travel by boat.

On the way to Rome a
terrible storm struck
Paul's ship. The entire
crew was very afraid!

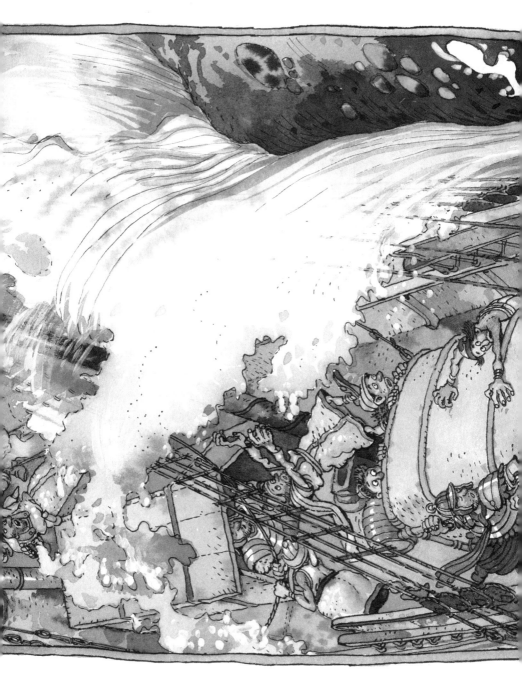

The storm raged and blew day after day, night after night. Some of the men wanted to jump off the ship, but Paul said, "Unless these men stay on the ship, they cannot be saved!"

Cup your hand around your mouth. Can you howl like the wind in a storm?

Finally the ship hit some rocks and started to break apart. "Abandon ship!" the captain called. Everyone jumped into the water and swam for the shore.

Call out, "Man overboard!" Now call it out as loud as you can, and remember to go UP AND DOWN at the same time.

Paul and everyone else on board swam safely to the island called Malta. The people there showed great kindness to the strangers from the storm. God had kept his promise.

Go and do one act of kindness for the person reading to you now.

Paul made it to Rome.
He was still under arrest and
had a Roman guard with him,
but he was free to go where he
pleased and talk about Jesus.

Can you find Rome on a map?

The more Paul talked to people about Jesus, the more often Jesus' enemies arrested and hurt Paul.

During his many years in jail, Paul wrote several letters to his friends.

Who does your family write letters to?

Paul started his journey as an enemy of Jesus. But Paul had a change of heart. He ended up traveling far and wide, spreading the Good News that Jesus lives and forgives!

A journey is a trip. On every trip, short or long, be sure to remember the Good News that Jesus loves you.

37

A NOTE TO THE big PEOPLE:

The *Little Children's Bible Books* may be your child's first introduction to the Bible, God's Word. This book about Paul is based on passages from the Book of Acts and Paul's Letters in the Bible. This is a DO book. Point things out and ask your child to find, seek, say, and discover.

Before you read these stories, pray that your child's little heart would be touched by the love of God. These stories are about planting seeds, having vision, learning right from wrong, and choosing to believe. Pray together after you read this. There's no better way for big people to learn from little people.

A little something fun is said in italics by the narrating animal to make the story come alive. In this DO book, wave, wink, hop, roar, or do any of the other things the stories suggest so this can become a fun time of growing closer.